LUFTWAFFE AT WAR

Focke Wulf 190
The Birth of the Butcher Bird
1939–1943

Focke Wulf 190A-3 'White 14' of 4.II./JG 2 'Richthofen'. The horizontal bar to the left of the *Balkenkreuz* indicates that it belongs to II. *Gruppe*, and the white number shows that it is from the 4. *Staffel*. The photo, taken in October 1942, is an original *Werkfoto* of Focke Wulf *Flugzeugbau GmbH* in Bremen. *(AG 11/2)*

LUFTWAFFE AT WAR

Focke Wulf 190
The Birth of the Butcher Bird
1939–1943

Morten Jessen

Greenhill Books
LONDON

Stackpole Books
PENNSYLVANIA

Greenhill Books

Focke Wulf 190: The Birth of the Butcher Bird, 1939–1943
first published 1998
by Greenhill Books, Lionel Leventhal Limited,
Park House, 1 Russell Gardens,
London NW11 9NN
and
Stackpole Books, 5067 Ritter Road, Mechanicsburg,
PA 17055, USA

British Library Cataloguing in Publication Data

Jessen, Morten
Focke Wulf 190: the birth of the Butcher Bird,
1939–1943. – (Luftwaffe at war; v. 8)
1. Focke-Wulf 190 (Fighter planes) – History 2. World
War, 1939–1945 – Aerial operations, German
I. Title
940.5'44'943
ISBN 1-85367-328-5

Library of Congress Cataloging-in-Publication Data

Jessen, Morten.
Focke Wulf 190: the birth of the Butcher Bird,
1939–1943/by Morten Jessen.
  p. cm. – (Luftwaffe at war; v. 8)
ISBN 1-85367-328-5
1. Focke-Wulf 190 (Fighter planes) 2. World War,
1939-1945–Aerial operations, German. I. Title.
II Series.
UG1242.F5J48 1998   98-17739
623.7'464'094309044-dc21   CIP

Designed by DAG Publications Ltd
Designed by David Gibbons
Layout by Anthony A. Evans
Printed in Singapore

FOCKE WULF 190

On 1 January 1924 the Focke Wulf *Flugzeug-bau AG* was founded by Heinrich Focke, George Wulf and Dr. Werner Naumann. They worked in a hangar at Bremen Airport, where the Focke Wulf company designed light aircraft and transports. It was not until 1 November 1931 that the designer of the Focke Wulf 190 entered the firm: *Diploma Ingenieur* (Diploma Engineer) Kurt Waldemar Tank who had worked for various other companies, including the *Bayerische Flugzeug AG* at Augsburg under Willy Messerschmitt.

In the spring of 1938 the Messerschmitt Bf 109 had just entered service, when the *Reichsluftfahrtministerium* (RLM) – the Air Ministry – asked the Focke Wulf company to begin designing proposals for an alternative fighter. Of the various designs, the Fw 190 was accepted. Kurt Tank, who had served in the cavalry and infantry during World War I, knew the conditions in which equipment had to operate during war. He wanted to create a full-blooded warhorse, easy to operate and maintain, but able to give and take a lot of punishment.

Approximately 19,000 Focke Wulf 190s were produced in various versions, compared with approximately 35,000 Bf 109s.

The Prototype

The Fw 190 design team consisted of about a dozen men. Two of them, Hans Sander and Kurt Melhorn, were test pilots and they were brought into the project early. They participated in the design, especially for the layout of the cockpit and the design and positioning of instruments. On 1 June 1939 Hans Sander flew the Fw 190V-1 on its maiden flight. It had good handling characteristics and the controls were well balanced, but the flight was not without problems. The temperature in the cockpit rose to 55°C and needless to say it was very uncomfortable for the pilot. The problem, caused because the cockpit was situated immediately behind the engine, was not solved until the V-5 model was built, when the heavier and more powerful BMW 801 engine replaced the smaller BMW 139, and the cockpit was moved back to compensate for the added weight.

During the test flights another problem arose. Above the speed of approximately 430 km/h aerodynamic forces made the canopy hood impossible to open by hand. This meant that a pilot could not get out in an emergency at high speed. Placing small explosive charges around the hood, which blew it away, solved the problem.

Tests with an ejector seat were conducted, but the results were not positive and the idea was abandoned.

In Operation

With the V-5 model the Fw 190 was ready for mass production, although there were still a lot of minor teething problems. The first Fw 190A-1 aircraft came off the production line from the factory at Marienburg by the end of July 1941. The *6. Staffel* of *Jagdgeschwader* 26 'Schlageter' was the first operational unit to test the new fighter under operational conditions. By September the entire II./JG 26 had been re-equipped.

On 26 September the first dogfight between a superior force of Spitfires and four Fw 190s, from the *6. Staffel* of JG 26, took place. It ended with three downed Spitfires and no German casualties. JG 2 'Richthofen' was the second *Jagdgeschwader* to re-equip with the Butcher Bird, as it also was called, in the spring of 1942. The Fw 190 was faster and more manoeuvrable than the Spitfire Mark V, the best fighter available to the RAF. The Fw 190's great speed meant that it could break off combat almost at will. The British were keen to examine the German fighter, and were delighted when, on 23 June 1941, *Oberleutnant* Arnim Faber of III./JG 2 landed his brand-new Fw 190A-3 at Pembrey Airfield, near Swansea. He had become disoriented after a short fight with Spitfires and mistook the Bristol Channel for the English Channel.

Fighter-Bomber

On 10 March 1942 General Sperrle ordered the two *Jagdgeschwadern* based in France to each form a *Jagdbomberstaffel* (fighter-bomber unit). JG 2 formed 10 Jabo/JG 2 equipped with the Bf 109F-4/R1. JG 26 formed 10 Jabo/JG 26, also equipped with the Bf 109F-4/R1 at first, and later re-equipped with the Fw 190A-4/U3 and U8. The A-4 was equipped with a methanol-water 50 power boost system to increase performance below 16,000 feet, which made it very useful during the low-level hit-and-run raids against the south coast of England. The U8 variant used for these attacks could carry two 250 litre auxiliary fuel tanks, and two 50 kg bombs on each wing rack or one 500 kg bomb on a fuselage rack. With all this auxiliary equipment it still carried full armament, consisting of two 7.92mm machineguns over the cowling, two 20mm machineguns in the wing roots and two 20mm machineguns in the outer wings.

The U8 was just one of several A-4 sub-variants used in the *Jabo* raids. The *Jabo* raids were performed at wave top height to avoid radar and to take the British targets by surprise. During 1942 and 1943 the British had to use a lot of resources (fighters and anti-aircraft guns) in order to protect the targets, because the Fw 190 came in so low the radar could not detect them. When Germans were spotted the Observer Corps reported them, but by the time the Spitfires were dispatched the Focke Wulfs had dropped their bombs and were on their way home at full throttle. The RAF had to mount standing patrols, which were tiring, expensive and inefficient, to counter the hit-and-run attacks. After these raids across the English Channel, the Fw 190 began to be deployed in the fighter-bomber role on all fronts.

The F and G Series

Now that the Fw 190 had proved its worth as a fighter-bomber, the Focke Wulf company began to design specific fighter-bomber variants, based on the Fw 190A-4/U8. The Fw 190 fighter-bomber was built to replace the Ju 87 *Stuka* as well as the Bf 109, after the Battle of Britain proved the Ju 87 to be too slow and vulnerable to single-engine fighters. The fighter-bomber models were split into two series, the F and the G series. The first F model, the F-1, was delivered at the end of 1942. It was based on the A-4 airframe, but differed from the fighter version by having its outboard guns removed and bomb racks installed. The F-2 followed shortly afterwards. This was the first model to feature a more spacious canopy like that of the Spitfire, which allowed the pilot to turn his head more easily and so increased his range of vision. Production was halted after approximately 550 F series aircraft had been produced, and the G model was produced instead. The G-1, G-2 and G-3 were also based on the A-4 and A-5 airframes. They were intended to be long range fighter-bombers and were designated as such: *Jagdbomber mit vergrösserter Reichweite (Jabo Rei)*. The G-4, G-5, G-6 and G-7 never reached front line service, but the G-8, which was similar to the A-8 fighter, was delivered to operational units. Production of the G-8 was terminated in February 1944 after more than 900 G models had left the assembly line. In the spring of 1944 the F-8, which had been developed in parallel, began to leave the factories.

Bomb Types

The differences between the F models and G models were relatively small. However it was possible to equip the fighter-bombers with a variety of bombs and auxiliary equipment. The bombs could be of different weight, size and shape, but basically there were three types of bombs, SC, SD and PC. The SC (*Sprengbombe Cylindrisch*) thin-walled, general purpose HE (high explosive) bomb was mainly used against soft targets, such as infantry and trucks. The SD (*Sprengbombe Dickwändig*) thick-walled, armour-piercing or semi-armour-piercing HE bomb was used against lightly armoured targets. The PC (*Panzersprengbombe Cylindrisch*) armour-piercing bomb was used against heavily protected targets. The colour on the fins identified the bomb type (SC bomb fins were yellow, SD fins red and PC fins blue). Later in the war the AB 250 bomb container was developed. It held numerous small SD-2, SD-4 or SD-10 bomblets, and was very useful against widely dispersed soft targets.

The Fw 190 served both as a dive-bomber and for low-level bombing attacks. Almost all *Schlachtgeschwadern* were equipped partly or wholly with Fw 190 Fs or Gs by the war's end.

The Eastern Front

On the Eastern Front the Fw 190 fighter-bomber versions were deployed with great success. Their task was to support the army forces on the ground. During the Russian offensives the *Schlachtgeschwadern* were especially useful in fighting the Russian break-throughs.

The *Schlachtgeschwadern* usually started the day with a reconnaissance mission, to find out where the enemy was. When the *Schlachtgeschwadern* attacked they aimed for the soft targets. They bombed fuel trucks, knowing that the tanks could not go far without fuel, and also targeted other trucks and lightly armoured vehicles. When the bombs had been dropped the guns and cannon were used on whatever was left. Tanks were only the primary target was if they were in contact with the German ground forces. These ground attack missions seldom lasted more than 30 to 60 minutes, because the *Schlachtgeschwadern* operated from forward airfields.

When the Fw 190 made its bomb run, it came in at 20–30 feet and at 480 km/h. As the target disappeared under the cowling the pilot released the bomb, which was set with a one-second-delay fuse. Sometimes the bomb bounced off the ground before hitting and exploding the target.

North Africa

On 8 November 1942 the Western allies launched operation Torch, a seaborne invasion to land 107,000 American and British troops on the coasts of Morocco and Algeria. Immediately after the enemy force had landed, III./ZG 2 was ordered to Tunisia. III./ZG 2 (III. *Gruppe* of *Zerstörergeschwader* 2) was the first *Zerstörer* (destroyer) unit to re-equip with Fw 190A-4 fighter-bombers, converting from Bf 109Es, which they had flown over Russia. Engaging in anti-shipping operations on the Allied supply ports in North Africa, they were met by a wall of flak and gunfire, and sometimes suffered heavy losses. The operations against the Allies, who were well equipped and well trained, were much more difficult than those against the Russians.

Colours and Markings

Thoughout the war camouflage schemes and markings changed as the battle fronts moved north, south and east. All types of aircraft had standard colour schemes, designed by the RLM and using standard RLM colours.

The early Fw 190As were delivered with a standard factory-painted colour scheme. The factory camouflage scheme consisted of RLM 02 *Grau* (grey) and RLM 71 *Dunkelgrün* (dark green) on the upper surfaces. The sides and under surfaces were painted RLM 65 *Hellblau* (light blue). Spinner and propeller were in RLM 70 *Schwarzgrün* ('black green'). Some time after the Fw 190 was made operational the camouflage colours were changed by the RLM. On the Eastern Front the sides of the aircraft were repainted in green colours after their transfer flight. Combat seldom took place higher than 10,000–12,000 feet, and the aircraft colours therefore needed to reflect the treetops and grassy fields. During the winter the aircraft would be painted all over with white water-based paint, except for the markings. In the spring, when the snow melted, the white paint was washed off and the original colours reappeared.

In the first two years of the war the colours were gloss and the ground crews spent hours polishing the surfaces of the aeroplanes. When the pilots discovered that the gloss surfaces reflected sunlight, which made them easier to spot, the polishing and gloss colours were abandoned.

Apart from the national *Balkenkreuz* and swastika, each *Geschwader* was identified by an emblem, usually painted on the engine cowling. Fighters and ground-attack units did not use the normal four-digit identification code, as they needed something that could be easily read during combat where everything was happening quickly. A *Jagdgeschwader* was split up into three or sometimes four *Gruppen*. Each *Gruppe* was identified by a symbol painted behind the fuselage cross, except for I. *Gruppe*, which had no symbol. II. *Gruppe* had a horizontal bar, III. *Gruppe* had a vertical bar and IV. *Gruppe* had a circle or a cross. Each *Gruppe* contained three *Staffeln*, which were identified by their own *Staffel*-colour. The individual *Staffel*-aircraft were given a number, which was painted forward of the fuselage cross in the *Staffel*-colour, and often outlined in black or white.

During the Spanish Civil War successful pilots began to paint victory bars on their aircraft. This continued in World War II, with little variation. Every time a pilot scored a victory a little vertical bar was painted on the rudder. Pilots who flew against more than one nationality often marked each bar with a national insignia, and the date of the victory. As the war progressed more and more aces appeared, and the rudder was filled with victory bars. To solve this problem medals were painted on the rudder as they were awarded, with the number of victories painted below. Then the pilot would start again, continuing to paint bars below the medal.

Acknowledgements

I would like to express my thanks to OSF Falk Hallensleben of JG 71 and to Chris 'Floyd' König, LV, of AG 11/JG 2 who both largely contributed with pictures to this book. I would also like to thank my friends Matt and Dubré for help and encouragement throughout the project.

Bibliography

Caldwell, Don, *The JG 26 War Diary* (Grub Street, 1996)

Campbell, Jerry L., *Focke Wulf 190 in Action* (Squadron Signal, 1975)

Nowarra, Heinz J., *Focke Wulf Fw 190 – Ta 152* (Motorbuch, 1987)

Price, Alfred, *Focke Wulf 190 at War* (Ian Allan, 1977)

Toliver, Raymond F. and Trevor J. Constable, *Fighter Aces of the Luftwaffe* (Schiffer, 1996)

Some of the early Fw 190s (left to right): Fw 190V-5, Fw 190V-2 (RM+CA), Fw 190A-0/U11 (WNr. 0015), Fw 190A-1 (KB+PJ) and Fw 190A-0/U4 (WNr. 0022). This photograph was probably taken in June 1941, when the first test flights with the A-1 took place. (AG 11/2)

Above: The Fw 190V-1 in the experimental workshop in the spring of 1939. In front the cooling fan for the air-cooled radial engine can be seen. Kurt Tank chose this type of engine because it was reliable and could take more punishment than liquid-cooled types. Liquid-cooled engines were more fragile, because if the cooling system were damaged, the engine overheated. Behind the tail, some Fw 189 canopies can be seen. *(Archiv Von Lutz)*

Below: Production minister Ernst Udet, one of the famous aces from World War I, inspecting the Fw 190V-1 prototype with *Generalingenieur* Lucht. This picture was taken in the summer of 1939 at Rechlin. *(Archiv Von Lutz)*

Above: A V-1 taxiing at Bremen airport. The two test pilots Hans Sanders (seen here at the controls) and Kurt Melhorn were both trained engineers. After the Focke Wulf 190 project Kurt Tank said that he would only use test pilots who were engineers. It was a tremendous help at the test flight debriefing if the pilot could express himself in technical terms and had an idea of what was causing a problem. *(Archiv Von Lutz)*

Below: The assembly line at the Marienburg works made early production batches of the machines. By the end of the war this number had grown, and the Fw 190 was produced at the rate of several hundred per month, to the surprise of the Allied Bomber Command, who thought they had destroyed the German aircraft industry. *(Archiv Von Lutz)*

Opposite page, top: Two brand-new Fw 190A-3s, which have just left the assembly line and are awaiting test flights before transferring to their operational units. Each aircraft was subjected to a standard test flight involving particular manoeuvres. This picture was taken in October 1942, at the Focke Wulf factory airfield in Bremen. *(AG 11/2)*

Opposite page, bottom: Among the many Luftwaffe pilots who flew the Fw 190 was Adolf Galland, seen here flanked by Werner Mölders (right) and Ernst Udet (left). Note the Oak Leaves to their Knight's Crosses. *(AG 11/2)*

Above: Taken from the German newspaper *Signal*, which was published throughout the war and known for its colour pictures, this picture shows Fw 190A-3 'White 14' from 1.I./JG 2 near the Channel coast, autumn 1942. Note the camouflage net on the wing. *(AG 11/2)*

Right: A line of Fw 190G-3s from 5. *Staffel* II./SG 2 'Immelmann', gathered at Deblin-Irena in Poland, in 1943. The squadron was commanded by *Major* Heinz Frank and the unit served most of its time on the Eastern Front. *(AG 11/2)*

The original small wing of the Fw 190V-5k – 'k' for *'kleine Fläche'*: small (wing) area – increased speed and rate of roll, but diminished the climb speed and manoeuvrability. On production aircraft a larger wing was fitted. *(Bundesarchiv 97/14/2A)*

Above: An Fw 190G-3 based at the Montecorvino airfield near Salerno just south of Naples, in 1943. It is equipped with a fuselage bomb rack and two ETC 501 V.Fw Trg (*Verkleideter Focke Wulf Träger*) underwing racks, which could carry either 300 litre fuel tanks or 250 kg bombs. Several Fw 190G-3s were captured at this airfield in 1943, when Allied troops occupied it on their way up through Italy. (*Jeff Ethell via James V. Crow*)

Below: This Fw 190 is an A-5/U8, which probably belonged to SKG 10 and was captured after the unit's retreat from Tunisia. It was captured in 1943 at Gerbini, Sicily by the 85th Fighter Squadron, 79th Fighter Group, USAAF, and was later tested by the U.S. Navy Tactical Test Division. It most likely ended up as scrap iron. (*James V. Crow*)

Above: An Fw 190A-1 is seen in its final stages of construction at the factory near Warnemünde in Mecklenburg-Vorpommern. One hundred Fw 190A-1s were produced before the A-2 model went into production. The A-2 was produced at the Warnemünde and Oschersleben works, because the factory near Warnemünde did not have sufficient capacity. The Arado *Flugzeugwerke GmbH* was also based near Warnemünde. In the beginning of their air activities, the Arado aircraft had to be sailed across the Warnow river by boat, because the factory had no airstrip. *(Archiv Von Lutz)*

Below: An Fw 190V-5k is being towed to its start position on the runway. It was tested carrying two Rheinmetal Borsig 7.92mm MG 17 machineguns mounted above the engine. This was the first Fw 190 to carry armament. Nine Fw 190V-5ks were built. *(Archiv Von Lutz)*

Opposite page bottom: A line of aircraft from the first A-1 production batch at the Marienburg works. In front is the eighth aircraft in the batch. *(Archiv Von Lutz)*

Left and below: The four-letter registration code painted on this newly built aircraft is 'SB-IA'. The factory-applied registration code (which would later be replaced by a military serial number) was painted on both sides of the fuselage and the under surface of the wing. This code is painted black, while others were painted white or light grey. This Fw 190A-1 is probably being prepared for the transfer flight to its operational unit in France. *(Archiv Von Lutz)*

Opposite page, top:
Among the six *Leutnant*-ranked officers pictured here are Bühligen and Bleymüller. Later in the war they became very capable and skilful fighter leaders. Kurt Bühligen became *Kommodore* of JG 2 'Richthofen' until the decommissioning of the Stab/JG 2. *Oberstleutnant* Bühligen managed to lead a few aircraft to Pocking (Bavaria), and he ordered the unit to disarm on 30 April 1945, at a farmhouse in Föching nearby. *(JG 71)*

Above: Close-up of a standard auxiliary drop tank, which fitted both the Bf 109 and Fw 190 and was used throughout the war. It could hold 300 litres of fuel, and was dropped just before combat so that it would not reduce the aircraft's speed and manoeuvrability. *(Archiv Von Lutz)*

Below: The reliable and powerful BMW 801 engine powered the Fw 190As throughout the war. It was frequently improved, and in 1945 the BMW 801F engine was developed, and would have powered the Fw 190A-9 if production had started in time. The BMW 801F produced approximately 2,400 hp on take-off and in emergencies, using methanol-water injection. *(Archiv Von Lutz)*

Right: An Fw 190A being readied for a flight. The bails of hay behind the aircraft served as camouflage, but gave no protection from gunfire or bomb splinters. *(Bundesarchiv 226/197/14A)*

Opposite page, top: Aircraft of the 6. *Staffel* of JG 2 'Richthofen' are being readied before action in 1942. This kind of line-up was only possible in the first half of the war. From mid-1944, aircraft had to be heavily camouflaged until just before take-off, to escape Allied aerial attacks. *(JG 71)*

Left: An Fw 190A-3 at the test field has its guns recalibrated and tested by the squadron's Technical Officer. This had to be done once in a while to ensure the accuracy of the guns, and to check the firing synchronization. *(Bundesarchiv 630/3586/3A)*

Above: *Unteroffizier* (corporal) Heinz Hanke leaning up against the cockpit of an Fw 190A-3 (WNr. 0495) in the spring of 1942. He joined 9.III./JG 1 when the *Staffel* was formed early in 1942. Hanke flew this aircraft, which was lent by Stab III./JG 1, on several occasions. His first flight in it was from Husum to Esbjerg in Denmark and back again, on 24 September 1942. On 26 September he flew an *Alarmstart* from Husum, and his final two flights in it were on 7 October 1942. *(Archiv Von Lutz)*

Below: Another picture of Heinz Hanke on his way out of the cockpit in 'Yellow 2'. This picture was taken in 1942, at Husum in northern Germany, when he was serving with the 9.III./JG 1. In April 1943 the unit was renamed to 3.I./JG 11 and Hanke stayed with it until he was transferred as a shooting instructor to a school where he ended the war. *(Junker)*

A moody soldier stands guard beside an early Fw 190A from III. *Gruppe* of a unit in northern France. *(Bundesarchiv 611/2129/21A)*

Left: This Fw 190A-3 of 10.III./JG 2 is based on an airfield somewhere in northern France in 1942. The characteristic eagle insignia of JG 2 is clearly visible on the cowling and fuselage. Aircraft of III./JG 2 were painted with either the eagle or a cockerel's head. It was not only a striking decoration: it also hid the exhaust stains which developed behind the louvres. *(James V. Crow)*

Opposite page, bottom: This Fw 190A-3, 'Yellow 3' of 7.II./JG 2, is flying somewhere over northern France in 1942. The fine performance of the Focke Wulf enabled it to enter and break off combat almost at will, which made it very popular with the German pilots. *(JG 71)*

Below: Albert Speer (left) and *Generalluftzeugmeister* (Director General of Equipment) Erhard Milch (right) inspect the radial engine of an Fw 190A. Milch began his military career in an artillery regiment in 1909. In 1915 he joined the Flying Service and flew with reconnaissance units, but ended up commanding the fighter squadron *Jagdgruppe 6*. In November 1941 he was promoted to *Generalluftzeugmeister* following the suicide of Ernst Udet. *(AG 11/2)*

50268

Opposite page, top: Walter Oesau of Stab/JG 2, in the summer of 1942. 'Gulle', as he was nicknamed, served with JG 51 when the war broke out. He was promoted to *Gruppenkommandeur* of II./JG 51 in August 1940 during the Battle of Britain, and went with the squadron to the Eastern Front in June 1941. In the east he scored 44 victories before returning to the west as *Kommodore* of JG 2 'Richthofen'. (*JG 71*)

Opposite page, bottom: The cockpit and guns of this Fw 190A-3 are being scrutinized intensively by several 'Black men' (slang for German ground crew, nicknamed for their black working overalls). Each time a model was improved the technicians had to learn about every change, so they could repair it properly. This aircraft belongs to II. *Gruppe* of an unidentified unit. (*JG 71*)

Above: New Fw 190F-1s are being rolled through the last check at the Oschersleben factory, before their test flights and subsequent transfer flights to an operational unit. The factory registration codes are clearly visible on the under surface of the wing and on the fuselage. (*Archiv Von Lutz*)

Below: This photograph shows Fw 190A-3 'Yellow 11' of 7.II./JG 2 in flight over the Channel in 1942. The A-3 was powered by the BMW 801D-2 which produced 1,700 hp at take-off. The engine cowling featured cooling louvres, which finally solved the heat problem. It was also the first A model which was able to use *Umrüst-Bausätze* (factory conversion sets), which could turn the Focke Wulf into a fighter-bomber or reconnaissance aircraft. (*JG 71*)

Left: Fw 190A-3 'Yellow 6' of 11.III./JG 2 based in northern France during the summer of 1942. The man beneath the aircraft is probably preparing it for a flight. *(JG 71)*

Below left: Assisted by ground personnel, the *Flugzeugführer* (pilot) of an Fw 190A-3 taxis his plane. The poor visibility from the cockpit made a guide necessary during taxiing before take-off and after landing. *(JG 71)*

Opposite page, top: An Fw 190A-3 or A-4 is being readied for flight. During 1942 the production of the Fw 190 rose rapidly. A total of 1,878 were produced during 1942, with a peak of 194 in June. The photo was released by Focke Wulf *Flugzeugbau*, Bremen, 10 October 1942. *(JG 71)*

Opposite page, bottom: This shot of an Fw 190A-3 was taken in France in 1942, when the Fw 190 was being used extensively only in the west. *(Bundesarchiv 367/2398/13A)*

Above: After air combat, pilots of III./JG 2 exchange combat experiences in front of a squadron aircraft. This picture was taken for propaganda purposes and the pilots were posed by the photographer. It was taken in the spring 1942 when the unit flew A-2s and A-3s. *(JG 71)*

Below: Although it had rather heavy lines when viewed from the side, the Fw 190 displayed slim lines from the front. This Fw 190A-3 belongs to JG 2 'Richthofen'. Behind the port wing is a small wooden flak tower. *(JG 71)*

Above: Early A models were commonly referred to as 'heavy smokers': leaked oil can be seen on the cooling louvres of this A-3. Having just returned from a flight, the pilot is being assisted out of the cockpit by one of his mechanics. The aircraft belongs to II./JG 2, pictured at Beaumont-le-Roger, France early in 1942. *(JG 71)*

Below: A mechanic warms up the engine before take-off. The camouflage scheme is standard for an early Fw 190A, except for the black paint over the exhaust area. This Fw 190A-3 belongs to 9.III./JG 2 which operated on the Western Front during most of the war. Note the aircraft's number, which is relatively high. *(Archiv Von Lutz)*

Opposite page: The cockerel's head and the red lower surface of the cowling indicate that the aircraft belongs to III./JG 2. *Major* 'Assi' Hahn introduced the badge (*Hahn* is German for cockerel). Posing in front of the aircraft are (left) an *Oberfeldwebel* (flight sergeant) and (right) a *Feldwebel* (sergeant). *(JG 71)*

Above: An Fw 190A-3 taking off from its base in northern France in 1942. The Fw 190A had to reach 180 km/h before it could become airborne. This particular aircraft served with JG 2, and the vertical bar on the left side of the *Balkenkreuz* indicates that it belonged to III. *Gruppe*. Note the exhaust beneath the aircraft. *(JG 71)*

Below: Probably the most famous Fw 190A-3: *Gruppen-adjutant Oberleutnant* Arnim Faber's aircraft, which he landed by mistake at Pembrey in South Wales. When Faber jumped out of his aircraft he was met by one Sergeant Jeffreys, who pointed his flare gun at Faber's head. After interrogation, Faber spent the rest of the war in a POW camp. *(Archiv Von Lutz)*

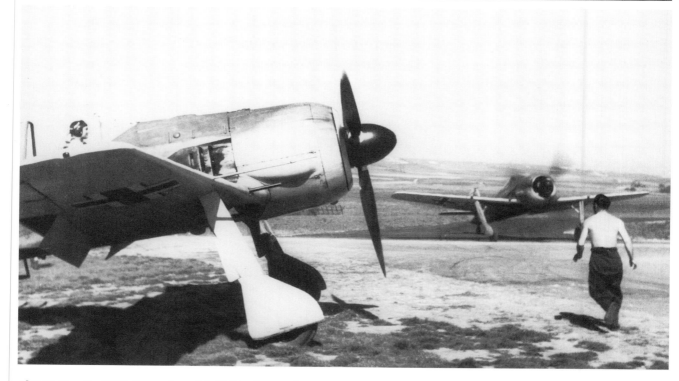

Above: Two Fw 190A-3s serving with JG 2 in France during the summer of 1942, probably about to take off for a channel patrol. The aircraft in the foreground is not yet ready: the canopy has not been closed and the retractable foot-step has not been pushed up. *(Bundesarchiv 604/1527/7)*

Below: The stamp on this photograph indicates that the picture, declared secret according to the *Reichsstrafgesetzbuch* (*Reich* Penal Code) dated 24 April 1944, had been released by the Fl. H. Kdtr. E 15/XII (*Fliegerhorstkommandantur* – airfield command) in 1942. It shows Fw 190A-3 'White 7' after a belly-landing. The propeller was still turning at the time, causing all three blades to bend. *(JG 71)*

Above: *Gruppenkommandeur* of II./JG 2 *Hauptmann* Karl-Heinz Greisert celebrates his birthday. With him are (left to right): Kurt Bühligen, *Leutnant* Horst Benno Krüger (the leader of 5. *Staffel*), Greisert and Vogel. Greisert was credited with 32 victories and won the *Deutscheskreuz*, and reached the rank of *Major* before he was killed on 22 July 1942. *(James V. Crow)*

Below: The first two Focke Wulfs in this line are A-3s, and the rest are probably A-3s as well. They are most likely from Erg.JGr.West (*Ergänzungs-Jagdgruppe West* – fighter reserve west) stationed in Cazaux, France, in 1942 or 1943. They are painted with a standard splinter/mottle 74/75/76 camouflage scheme. *(Bundesarchiv 614/2446/23)*

Opposite page, top: Fw 190A-3 (WNr. 1460) of III./JG 51 in Russia during winter 1942/43. This aircraft, 'Red 1', was one of the first Fw 190s to be tested in the east. During the winter most aircraft were painted with water-based white paint all over as winter camouflage. In the spring when the snow began to melt the paint was washed off, if rain and snow had not removed it already. *(James V. Crow)*

Opposite page, bottom: JG 51 'Mölders' was the first *Jagdgeschwader* to test the Fw 190 under the harsh conditions on the Eastern Front in 1941/42. It was not until late 1943 that it was used by JG 54 'Grünherz' as a fighter and by *Schlachtgeschwadern* (ground-attack units) as a fighter-bomber. This Fw 190A-3 belongs to I./JG 51. The squadron emblem, the Icelandic falcon, and the emblem from I. *Gruppe*, are visible on the side of the aircraft. *(James V. Crow)*

Below: A mechanic closes one of the lower hatches of the engine after repairs or inspection. The ground crews worked day and night to keep as many aircraft as possible operational. Work conditions were tough during the Russian winter when the temperature could fall to –50°C. These Fw 190As are from I./JG 54 on the Eastern Front during winter 1942/43. *(Bundesarchiv 625/3156/11A)*

Opposite page: Fw 190A-3s of JG 2 'Richthofen', stationed in northern France. The ground power supply is plugged into the fuselage of the aircraft in the foreground. *(Bundesarchiv 619/2664/7)*

Below: A member of the ground personnel directs the pilot to a halt. The aircraft is an Fw 190A-3 or A-4, operating on the Eastern Front with an unidentified unit. *(Bundesarchiv 517/83/36A)*

Above: A I./JG 51 Fw 190A-3 is refuelled and re-armed prior to a combat mission, in the primitive conditions under which the ground personnel had to work. From 1 June to 14 December 1942 this *Gruppe* was led by *Hauptmann* Heinrich 'Gaudi' Krafft until he was shot down. He bailed out, and was killed by Russian troops when he landed. Krafft shot down 78 aircraft, four of them in the west. *(James V. Crow)*

Below: An Fw 190A-3 of III./JG 51 'Mölders' has its engine changed on the field at the *Gruppe*'s base at Swzeskaya, Crimea, in early 1942. *(James V. Crow)*

Opposite page, top: This Fw 190A-3 or A-4 is being pushed to its camouflaged dispersal point after a flight. The aircraft belongs to JG 26 'Schlageter' and it is pictured somewhere in northern France, in the summer of 1942. (*Bundesarchiv 604/1523/21*)

Right: A pilot of III./JG 2 poses in front of his Fw 190A-3. The lower cowling is probably red, which signifies III. *Gruppe* JG 2 'Richthofen'. (*JG 71*)

Opposite page, bottom: This Fw 190A-3 or A-4 belongs to JG 26 'Schlageter', and is pictured here in the summer of 1942. (*Bundesarchiv 604/1523/36*)

Below: An early Fw 190A in the foreground, in front of another that has had its engine removed. Both are painted with very irregular camouflage schemes and belong to I. *Gruppe* of an unidentified unit. A Messerschmitt Bf 109E can be seen just behind the Fw 190 numbered '23'. (*Bundesarchiv 625/3171/23*)

Above: A pilot of III./JG 2 aircraft and a crewmember, who is leaning up against the cockpit, await the orders for take-off. At this point of 'cockpit readiness' the ground crew had to be close, so that they could assist the pilot and make the final checks. *(Bundesarchiv 604/1542/27)*

Below: *Major* Hahn in the cockpit of his aircraft, preparing for another combat mission over the English Channel. He scored two victories in his first air battle on 14 May 1940, and won 108 confirmed victories during the war, 40 of which were downed in the east with II./JG 54. *(JG 71)*

Above and below: The pilot of this Fw 190A-3, 'Black 3', was *Oberfähnrich* Terborg. He served with 5.II./JG 1, which was stationed at Katwijk in Holland during April and May 1942 when these two pictures were taken. At the end of July the *Staffel* was transferred to Schipol and the rest of II./JG 1 to Venlo and Deelen. The *Tatzelwurm* ('dragon-worm', a Nordic mythological creature), the *Gruppe* emblem, is visible on the engine cowling. The aircraft has a splinter/mottle 71/02/65 standard camouflage scheme. *(Bundesarchiv 361/2193/29 and 361/2193/25)*

Above: Hans 'Assi' Hahn's personal aircraft. Hahn was the well known *Staffelkapitän* of 4. *Staffel* in JG 2 during the early stages of the Battle of Britain. He served with both JG 2 'Richthofen' and II./JG 54 'Grünherz', and ended his career on the Eastern Front. He was shot down on 21 February 1943 and spent seven years in Soviet prison camps. (*JG 71*)

Opposite page, top: This Fw 190A-3 of JG 2 is being pushed out of its camouflaged hangar to the runway, where the 'Black men' would warm up the engine and make the last checks before take-off. Note the painting on the wing leading-edge, in addition to its factory camouflage scheme. (*Bundesarchiv 630/3586/9A*)

Right: These three Fw 190A-3s have reached the runway, and the first is having its engine warmed up by a mechanic. Standing out in the open and without any kind of additional camouflage these aircraft would be easily spotted during an air raid. They would remain vulnerable until they were in the air and had gained height and cruising speed. Note the non-standard painting on the wing leading-edge and lower part of the cowling. (*Bundesarchiv 369/2502/3*)

Opposite page, top: An Fw 190A-4 of I./JG 1, after crash-landing near Arnhem, 1942. The right undercarriage leg failed during the landing while the propeller was still turning, causing the blades to bend. The checked pattern on the cowling was later abandoned by JG 1, because the Americans also used it. I./JG 1 used checks in black/white, II./JG 1 black/red and III./JG 1 black/yellow. (*Archiv Von Lutz*)

Opposite page, bottom: An Fw 190A-3 seen through the rear cockpit glass of an Fw 189 'Uhu' reconnaissance aircraft. The picture was released for propaganda purposes on 18 August 1942 by the *Focke Wulf Bilderdienst*. In the original photograph, the Fw 190 carries guns in the wing, but on this print they have been erased by the censor. (*Bundesarchiv 97/8/3*)

Above: The date and location of these two Fw 190A-4s or A-3s, which have crashed while taxiing, remain unknown. This kind of accident sometimes killed the pilots involved. The pilot in the aircraft on the left probably escaped unharmed. The original photograph was released by Fl. H. Kdtr. E 25/XII in the summer of 1942. (*JG 71*)

Below: This Fw 190A-4, captured intact, has been shipped to the USA for closer examination. The radial engine, used in most carrier based aircraft, was of great interest to the Americans. It was not as long as the in-line engine and so did not take up as much space. (*Archiv Von Lutz*)

Opposite page, top: A 'Black man' looks though a gun barrel while cleaning it. This had to be done so that fragments of the projectiles did not build up in the barrel, making the machinegun inaccurate and unstable. The wing root MG 151 could be removed by rotating the barrel one-sixteenth of a turn, but had to be recalibrated every time it had been cleaned. *(Bundesarchiv 515/34/12)*

Opposite page, bottom: These pilots of 2./JG 2, in northern France in 1943, are being briefed by their *Staffelführer* prior to a sortie. *(JG 71)*

Right: Vapour trails from the aeroplanes leave an impression of how chaotic an air battle was: only skilful pilots had a chance to get an overview of the 'battlefield'. Air battles were usually very intense, lasting only a few minutes before the fighting went on in smaller groups or pairs. Tactics also depended a lot upon the enemy's position, strength and type (fighter versus fighter, fighter versus bomber and so on). *(Bundesarchiv 602/1210/32)*

Below: A 'Black man' guides a pilot taxiing his plane. This Fw 190A-4/U3 has probably just landed after a *Jabo* (*Jagdbomber* – fighter-bomber) mission over southern England in the summer of 1942. These raids were very effective, and were carried out with minimum loss because the British fighters often failed to intercept. *(James V. Crow)*

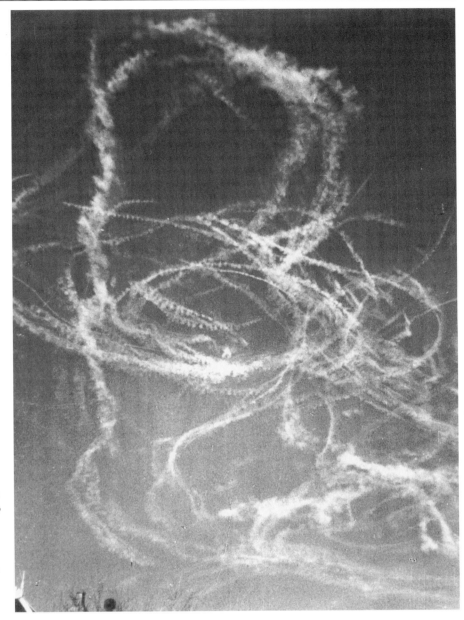

Left: A *Wart* (ground crew) helps a pilot adjust his parachute, somewhere in Russia. The aircraft they are standing on cannot be identified as a particular model. It has the cooling louvres of an A-4, and the wingroot fillet of an A-5 and later models. It is probably an A-5, which has had its cowling fuselage around the cooling louvres replaced during repairs. (*AG 11/2*)

Opposite page: This Fw 190 is having its engine removed by the tool hanging just over the cowling. Before this could be done the propeller and the armoured ring in front of the engine had to be removed as well. (*Bundesarchiv 603/1289/11*)

Above: A Fw 190F-2 trop ('tropical version') waits to be ferried to its operational unit. Machines such as this saw service both in the Mediterranean and on the dusty steppe of the southern sector of the Russian Front, where they were engaged in ground support for the army. Note the closed tropical filters and fuselage rack for a drop tank. *(Archiv Von Lutz)*

Opposite page, top: An Fw 190A-4 of II./JG 2 in Tunisia. The *Gruppe* was sent from France to Tunisia in November 1942, but was called back in March 1943. Among the pilots in the *Gruppe* were *Oberstleutnant* Kurt Bühligen and *Leutnant* Erich Rudorffer, who won 40 and 27 victories here respectively. *(JG 71)*

Right: An Fw 190A-4 of JG 54 on the Eastern Front being prepared for a mission. The ice- and snow-covers have been removed and lie just beneath and behind each wing. Horses were often used as local means of transportation to conserve fuel. Also, fuel froze in winter temperatures of –30°C to –40°C, rendering vehicles and aircraft useless. *(Bundesarchiv 625/3194/30)*

Left: An Fw 190A from I./JG 54 taxis past parked aircraft. The pilot wears white headgear, matching the winter camouflage. These aircraft belong to I./JG 54 'Grünherz' based on the Eastern Front during winter 1942/43. *(Bundesarchiv 625/3156/9A)*

Opposite page, bottom: With landing gear and flaps down, this I./JG 54 aircraft returns from a mission over the Eastern Front. In the summer of 1942 the Russians began to outnumber the Germans, but superior tactics and skills made the German pilots successful against their poorly trained Russian counterparts. *(Bundesarchiv 625/3194/13)*

Below: This Fw 190A-4 of JG 54 has just landed on a thawing airstrip. When the temperature rose and the snow began to melt, the ground turned to mud, making take-off and landing more dangerous. *(Bundesarchiv 459/144/18)*

Above: Two *Schwärme* of Focke Wulfs fly in
their four-plane formations. On the ground an
Fw 190 fighter-bomber prepares for flight. The
ice- and snow-covers have been removed and
the aircraft carries a 500 kg bomb.
(Bundesarchiv 500/103/11)

Right: This Fw 190A-4 of II./JG 54 is being
serviced somewhere on the Eastern Front in
1943, where all aircraft were painted with
yellow wing tips and a yellow band around the
fuselage. For four months from 19 November
1942, *Hauptmann* (subsequently *Major*) Hahn
was the *Gruppenkommandeur* of II./JG 54.
(Bundesarchiv 459/140/16A)

Opposite page, top: A Russian Ilyushin Il-2
'Sturmovik' has fallen to German guns. It was
the ground-attack aircraft most commonly used
by the Russians and approximately 35,000 were
produced during the war. Armour plates to
protect the pilot, engine and cooling system,
which made it very difficult to shoot down,
accounted for fifteen per cent of the total
weight. The German pilots, flying Fw 190s and
Bf 109s, had to get as close as 100 metres
before their cannon had any effect on the
'Cementers'. *(Bundesarchiv 518/122/32)*

Opposite page, top: The double chevrons on this Fw 190A-5 or A-6 show that the aircraft belongs to a *Geschwaderkommodore*. Here Kurt Bühligen, *Kommodore* of JG 2, leaves his personal aircraft after a mission. Bühligen survived the war as an *Oberstleutnant* (wing commander or lieutenant-colonel), with 112 confirmed kills, including 24 *Viermot* (four-engine bombers). (*JG 71*)

Above: Anti-aircraft guns were as much part of the airfield as the hangars and barracks. Here the crew for a 20mm *flakvierling* (quadruple-barrelled anti-aircraft gun) runs into position during an air raid or a training exercise. This gun fired 800 rounds per minute, had a firing range of two miles and was effective against low flying aircraft. (*Bundesarchiv 602/1233/16*)

Left: 'Black 8' of 2.I./JG 54 is serviced at a large airfield with proper repair facilities during the spring of 1943. Most airfields on the Eastern Front were primitive advanced fields, without possibilities for making major repairs. In the background a winter camouflaged Fiesler Fi 156 'Storch' is parked. This was successfully used as a liaison and observation aircraft, known for its remarkable take-off and landing abilities. (*Bundesarchiv 461/221/6*)

Above: This new Fw 190A-5/U2 stands in front of the factory hangar waiting for its transfer flight. The U2 variant was intended as a *Nacht Jabo Rei* (long range night fighter-bomber). The two auxiliary fuel tanks could contain 300 litres each. Flame guards were installed around the cooling louvres. *(AG 11/2)*

Left: *Leutnant* Heinz-Günther Lück in his personal aircraft, an Fw 190A-4 'White 9', while serving with 1.I./JG 1, stationed in Deelen, Holland, September 1943. *(Archiv Von Lutz)*

Below: A mechanic surveys a damaged Fw 190 fighter-bomber. The pilot was lucky that he was not killed, as several rounds have hit the canopy. The white band indicates that this aircraft operated in the Mediterranean, probably in 1943. The markings on the side indicate that the aircraft belonged to the *Geschwader IA* (Operations officer) of an early *Schlachtgeschwader*. *(Bundesarchiv 332/3094/20)*

Above: An Fw 190A-3 or A-4 is loaded with a 250 kg bomb. Anything weighing more than 50 to 60 kg had to be loaded with a hydraulically operated carriage. The heavier bombs weighed 100, 250 and 500 kg. Here some 'Black men' are using a carriage in either Norway or Russia, during winter 1942/43. *(Bundesarchiv 634/3874/26)*

Below: A 'Black man' warms up an Fw 190A-4/U8 prior to a *Jabo* mission. The aircraft carries an ETC 501 fuselage bomb rack, which is loaded with a 500 kg bomb, and also carries

two 300 litre auxiliary fuel tanks. This was a common configuration for a long range fighter-bomber mission. *(Archiv Von Lutz)*

Right: A *Feuerwerker* (demolition expert) fuses a bomb in Russia, in 1943 or 1944. Two young trainee *Feuerwerkern* (the one to the left is ranked *Unteroffizier* – corporal) are being instructed by an *Oberfeldwebel* (flight sergeant) about how to handle the bomb. *(AG 11/2)*

Opposite page: An Fw 190A-4/U3 takes off loaded with a 500 kg bomb during the summer of 1942. It probably belongs to 10 Jabo/JG 26 and is heading for southern England. The A-4/U-3 variant was later improved and became the Fw 190F-1 fighter-bomber. *(Bundesarchiv 623/3039/10A)*

Above: The map of the Russian Front is studied in detail during the planning of an air operation. Front lines moved forwards and backwards almost daily, and every mission had to be planned with the current conditions in mind. If there was no information available a reconnaissance flight was ordered. *(Bundesarchiv 500/104/21)*

Left: Fw 190A-4 'White 7' of III./JG 54 being prepared for removal after a forced landing. For some reason the armoured plate behind the pilot's head has been removed. At the time this photograph was taken *Hauptmann* 'Seppl' Seiler commanded III. *Gruppe.* He took over command on 1 October 1941 after leaving the military hospital in Calais. He had been badly injured during combat in the Battle of Britain. *(Bundesarchiv 518/116/22)*

Above: A member of the ground crew poses in front of an Fw 190F-2 trop of I./SG 4, based in central Italy. The unit had a hard time, because most of the Luftwaffe fighter force was withdrawn to Germany to participate in the *Reichsverteidigung* (defence of the Reich) by the end of 1943, and there was usually no fighter escort. They were also outnumbered most of the time and fighting against a well trained enemy. *(Bundesarchiv 94/65/24)*

Opposite page, top: This Fw 190F has just lifted off the ground with a 250 kg bomb. The black triangle on the fuselage indicates that the aircraft belongs to *Schlachtgeschwader* (Schl.G) 1 or 2. The F and G models replaced the Ju 87 'Stuka' as ground-attack and close-support aircraft during 1943 and 1944. The Fw 190 fighter-bombers had additional armour around the cockpit and

lower cowling to protect against small arms fire and anti-aircraft guns. *(Bundesarchiv 333/3104/16A)*

Opposite page, bottom: This mechanic, serving with *Gefechtsverband* (battle unit) 'Druschel', takes a well earned nap between missions during the battle of Kursk in July 1943. The ground crew worked hard, sometimes more than twelve hours per day, seven days per week. Leave was not given without good reason, and a combat ready aircraft was not reason enough. When the work with the aircraft was finished the ground crew were often given other duties, such as standing guard. The 'C' above the *Geschwader Adjutant* marking on this Fw 190 refers to this specific aircraft within the *Staffel*, and is painted in a smaller size to allow room for the marking below it. *(Bundesarchiv 353/1639/31)*

Above: An Fw 190G-3 of 7.III./SKG 10 in Algiers in 1943. The Fw 190 was never widely used in North Africa, although it was potentially a good fighter-bomber. When it first arrived in North Africa, it was used in anti-shipping operations and attacks on the Allied harbours. *James V. Crow)*

Below: A captured Fw 190G-3 in North Africa in 1943. It was not only soldiers that were captured: large quantities of vehicles, aircraft and other military equipment were left behind when the Germans surrendered. Here an Allied soldier poses in front of an abandoned aircraft. Note the large white number '10' just visible on the tail, an unusual position for an individual aircraft number. *(James V. Crow)*

Above and below: Two photographs of the same Fw 190 fighter-bomber (WNr. 2308), probably a G-3, in Allied hands at La Sebala, Tunisia, in June 1943. The swastikas and *Balkenkreuz* have both been over-painted with some kind of unofficial marking (possibly the French tricolore). *(James V. Crow)*

Left: Two Fw 190F-2s serving with *Gefechtsverband* 'Druschel' on the Eastern Front. The wheel covers have been removed to prevent mud building up. The unit was named after *Oberst* Alfred Druschel, one of the most experienced ground-attack pilots in the Luftwaffe, who was killed on 1 January 1945. *(Bundesarchiv 353/1641/31)*

Below: The *Tatzelwurm* on the cowling was the emblem of I./JG 3, which later became II./JG 1. The colour of the *Tatzelwurm* differed for each *Staffel*. The right flap of this aircraft is half-way down and the pilot is probably about to leave the aircraft, indicating that he has just returned from a mission. *(Bundesarchiv 503/213/17)*